The Story of Christmas

by Martina Smith

illustrated by Peter Grosshauser
and Ed Temple

SPARK
HOUSE
FAMILY

MINNEAPOLIS

Once there was a faithful young woman named Mary. She lived about 2,000 years ago in a town called Nazareth. She was engaged to be married to a man named Joseph. One day an angel appeared in front of Mary.

"Hello, Mary," the angel said. "God is with you. Don't be afraid. God sent me to tell you that you will have a son. You will name him Jesus, and he will be very important to many people."

"But I'm not married yet," Mary said. "How is this going to happen?"

"The Holy Spirit will come to you," the angel replied. "Your son will be the Son of God."

3

When Mary told Joseph about giving birth to God's Son, he didn't believe her. But Mary remembered what the angel had said, and she trusted God.

The next day, Joseph told Mary, "An angel came to me in a dream! He told me, 'Don't be afraid. Make Mary your wife. She will have a son, and you will name him Jesus. He's going to save people from their sins.'"

Mary smiled a big smile. She was so happy that tears of joy filled her eyes and trickled down her cheeks. She felt Joseph's love again.

"I am not scared for you to be my wife, Mary," he said. "I will be with you, and we will name the boy Jesus."

One day Mary went to visit her cousin Elizabeth. Elizabeth was going to have a baby, and Mary wanted to tell her that she was going to have a baby too.

"Hello, Elizabeth!" Mary called.

The sound of Mary's voice made the baby inside Elizabeth wiggle with joy! Without even asking, Elizabeth knew the secret Mary wanted to tell her.

Elizabeth hugged Mary warmly and said, "Mary, God has blessed you more than any other woman, and God has blessed the baby you will have."

Mary was full of joy. "From now on, all people will know that God has blessed me and that God's name is holy. God has kept the promises made to the people of Israel."

One day, when it was nearly time for Mary to have the baby, Joseph said, "We have to go to Bethlehem. The emperor has ordered that all of the people need to be counted."

"But Joseph," Mary said, "what about our baby? He will be born soon."

"We'll go slowly, Mary. Bethlehem will be crowded, so we need to leave now."

So Mary and Joseph journeyed to Bethlehem
to be counted along with all of the other people.
It was cold when they arrived. Joseph knocked on
many doors looking for a room, but everyone said
no. Finally an innkeeper answered his door.

"I have no room," the innkeeper said. "But you can stay in the little stable in the back. It's warm, and the hay is fresh."

"Joseph," Mary said, "I think it's time for the baby to be born."

That night Mary gave birth to Jesus. She laid him in a manger.

Outside of Bethlehem, shepherds watched their sheep on the hills. Suddenly an angel appeared.

"Don't be afraid," the angel said. "I bring wonderful news. The child God promised was born tonight. Go to Bethlehem! You will find the child lying on a bed of hay."

The shepherds were amazed. Suddenly many angels filled the heavens. They sang, "*Glory to God in the highest. And peace to all people on Earth.*"

"Let's hurry!" one shepherd said.

The shepherds found the baby, Jesus, asleep on a bed of hay. The shepherds told Mary and Joseph, "The angel said the baby is the Messiah— the promised one. He is the one we have waited for. But this is a stable. Would this special child be born here among the animals?"

Mary smiled. She knew that Jesus was Immanuel—God with us.

Later the shepherds returned to their sheep, praising God for all they had seen and heard.

After the night Jesus was born, three wise men looked into the clear evening sky and saw a bright star. The wise men had been waiting for a king to come into the world.

"The star is a sign that the king has been born! We should follow the star to find him," one of the wise men said.

They left their homes and traveled far to meet this new baby king. They wanted to worship him and give him gifts.

Along the way, they stopped and visited King Herod, the ruler of that land. When King Herod heard that the baby king had been born, he worried that the baby would grow up and take over his kingdom.

So King Herod pretended to be nice, as he said to the wise men, "Why don't you find him and then come back here and tell me where he is? Then I can worship him too."

The wise men followed the star and found baby Jesus in Bethlehem. They gave him gifts of gold, frankincense, and myrrh. These expensive gifts were fit for a king.

Jesus was indeed a new baby king who was God's promise born for us—a gift to all people.

After meeting baby Jesus, the wise men had a dream warning them not to trust Herod, so they traveled home on a different road.

More Stories about Young Jesus

Escape to Egypt

After Jesus was born, an angel told Joseph in a dream that Jesus was in danger because of King Herod. The angel said they should go to Egypt to hide. The family went to Egypt, and God kept them safe. Later an angel told Joseph the family should go back to Israel. Then in another dream, an angel said to move to Nazareth. The family hurried to Nazareth and made their home there.

Young Jesus at the Temple

Jesus' family traveled to Jerusalem to celebrate the festival of Passover. The year that Jesus was 12, Mary and Joseph could not find him on the way home. They searched for three days. Finally they found him in the temple in Jerusalem, talking with teachers more than twice his age. The teachers were impressed by Jesus' wisdom. Jesus said to Mary and Joseph, "Didn't you understand that I was in my Father's house?"

Making Faith Connections: A Note to Adults

Sharing a Bible story with a child can be a wonderful time to grow your faith together. Here are a few suggestions for ways you can enrich a child's engagement and learning with this book.

Questions for Reflection

After reading the story together, ask your child these questions.

 How do you think the shepherds felt when they saw the angel? When they found baby Jesus?

 When you have exciting news to share, how do you tell your family or friends?

 If Jesus was born today, what gifts would you give to him?

Activities

 The wise men brought gifts for Jesus. Today we share gifts with each other to celebrate Christmas. Help your child make a gift for someone special. Draw a picture, make a clay sculpture, or string buttons into a necklace.

 Did you notice Squiggles, the expressive caterpillar who appears throughout the book? When you see Squiggles, after you read the text aloud, ask your child how

Squiggles is feeling. Then ask why Squiggles feels that way. Invite the child to share about a time they felt the same way Squiggles does.

 Sing this song together to the tune of "Twinkle, Twinkle, Little Star."

Twinkle, twinkle, star above
Baby Jesus, gift of love
Comes to Earth to show the way
God wants us to live each day
Twinkle, twinkle, star above
Baby Jesus, gift of love

Bible Connections

This picture book is based on the Bible texts in Matthew 1:18-25 and 2:1-23, as well as Luke 1:26-58 and 2:1-20, 41-52.

Bible Verse to Remember

Share this key Bible verse with your child and help him or her learn it. Refer to it at later times when it seems appropriate, as a reminder of the story you've shared together.

[Mary] gave birth to her firstborn son and wrapped him in bands of cloth, and laid him in a manger.
—Luke 2:7

24 23 22 21 20 19 18 17 16 15   1 2 3 4 5 6 7 8

Hardcover ISBN: 978-1-5064-0224-6

E-book ISBN: 978-1-5064-0225-3

Cover design: Alisha Lofgren
Book design: Eileen Z. Engebretson

Library of Congress Cataloging-in-Publication Data
Cataloging information on file with the Library of Congress

Printed on acid-free paper

Printed in U.S.A.

V63474; 9781506402246; OCT2015